Common Core Connections
Language Arts
Grade 2

Carson-Dellosa Publishing, LLC
Greensboro, North Carolina

Credits
Content Editor: Jeanette M. Ritch, MS. Ed.
Copy Editor: Julie B. Killian

 Visit *carsondellosa.com* for correlations to Common Core, state, national, and Canadian provincial standards.

Carson-Dellosa Publishing, LLC
PO Box 35665
Greensboro, NC 27425 USA
carsondellosa.com

ISBN 978-1-62442-043-6

03-104141151

Table of Contents

Introduction

What are the Common Core State Standards for Language Arts?

The standards are a shared set of expectations for each grade level in the areas of reading, writing, speaking, listening, and language. They define what students should understand and be able to do. The standards are designed to be more rigorous and allow for students to justify their thinking. They reflect the knowledge that is necessary for success in college and beyond.

As described in the Common Core State Standards, students who master the standards in reading, writing, speaking, listening, and language as they advance through the grades will exhibit the following capabilities:

1. They demonstrate independence.
2. They build strong content knowledge.
3. They respond to the varying demands of audience, task, purpose, and discipline.
4. They comprehend as well as critique.
5. They value evidence.
6. They use technology and digital media strategically and capably.
7. They come to understand other perspectives and cultures.*

How to Use This Book

This book is a collection of practice pages aligned to the Common Core State Standards for English Language Arts and appropriate for second grade. Included is a skill matrix so that you can see exactly which standards are addressed on the practice pages. Also included are a skill assessment and a skill assessment analysis. Use the assessment at the beginning of the year or at any time of year you wish to assess your students' mastery of certain standards. The analysis connects each test item to a practice page or set of practice pages so that you can review skills with students who struggle in certain areas.

Common Core State Standards*
Alignment Matrix

Pages	12	13	14	15	16	17	18	19	20	21	22	23	24	25	26	27	28	29	30	31	32	33	34	35	36	37	38	39	40	41	42	43	44	45	46	47	48	49	50
2.RL.1		●																																					
2.RL.2			●		●																																		
2.RL.3						●																																	
2.RL.4							●	●																															
2.RL.5									●																														
2.RL.6									●	●																													
2.RL.7											●																												
2.RL.9													●																										
2.RL.10	●			●								●		●	●																								
2.RI.1																●																							
2.RI.2																	●																						
2.RI.3																		●											●										
2.RI.4																			●				●																
2.RI.5																					●	●																	
2.RI.6																						●																	
2.RI.7																							●			●		●											
2.RI.8																								●															
2.RI.9																									●														
2.RI.10																●	●		●				●		●	●			●	●									
2.RF.3																															●								
2.RF.3a																																●	●		●				
2.RF.3b																																		●	●				
2.RF.3c																																				●			
2.RF.3d																																					●		
2.RF.3e																																						●	
2.RF.3f				●																																			●
2.RF.4																																							
2.RF.4a										●																													
2.RF.4b																																							
2.RF.4c																																							
2.W.1																																							
2.W.2																																							
2.W.3																																							
2.W.5																																							
2.W.6																																							
2.W.7																																							
2.W.8																																							
2.L.1																																							
2.L.1a																																							
2.L.1b																																							
2.L.1c																																							
2.L.1d		●																																					
2.L.1e																																							
2.L.1f																																							
2.L.2																																							
2.L.2a																																							
2.L.2b																																							
2.L.2c																																							
2.L.2d																																							
2.L.2e																																							
2.L.3								●																															
2.L.3a																																							
2.L.4																																							
2.L.4a																																							
2.L.4b																																				●			
2.L.4c														●																									
2.L.4d																																							
2.L.4e																																							
2.L.5																																							
2.L.5a																																							
2.L.5b																										●													
2.L.6																																							

© Carson-Dellosa • CD-104609

Common Core State Standards*
Alignment Matrix

Pages	51	52	53	54	55	56	57	58	59	60	61	62	63	64	65	66	67	68	69	70	71	72	73	74	75	76	77	78	79	80	81	82	83	84	85	86	87	88	89	90
2.RL.1																																								
2.RL.2																																								
2.RL.3																																								
2.RL.4																																								
2.RL.5																																								
2.RL.6																																								
2.RL.7																																								
2.RL.9																																								
2.RL.10																																								
2.RI.1																																								
2.RI.2																																								
2.RI.3																																								
2.RI.4																																								
2.RI.5																																								
2.RI.6																																								
2.RI.7																																								
2.RI.8																																								
2.RI.9																																								
2.RI.10			•					•																																
2.RF.3																																								
2.RF.3a																																								
2.RF.3b																																								
2.RF.3c																																								
2.RF.3d																																								
2.RF.3e																																								
2.RF.3f																																								
2.RF.4	•																																							
2.RF.4a		•		•																																				
2.RF.4b		•																																						
2.RF.4c			•																																					
2.W.1					•	•																																		
2.W.2						•																																		
2.W.3										•					•	•	•																							
2.W.5									•	•	•	•	•	•			•																							
2.W.6														•				•																						
2.W.7																			•	•		•																		
2.W.8																				•	•	•																		
2.L.1					•	•		•				•																												
2.L.1a																							•																	
2.L.1b																								•																
2.L.1c																									•															
2.L.1d																																								
2.L.1e																					•																			
2.L.1f			•																							•														
2.L.2																											•													
2.L.2a																												•												
2.L.2b																													•											
2.L.2c																														•										
2.L.2d																															•									
2.L.2e																																•								
2.L.3																																								
2.L.3a														•	•																									
2.L.4																																	•	•						
2.L.4a																																	•	•						
2.L.4b																																								
2.L.4c																																								
2.L.4d																																			•					
2.L.4e																																				•				
2.L.5																																					•			
2.L.5a																																						•		
2.L.5b																																							•	
2.L.6																																								•

Read the story. Answer each question with a complete sentence.

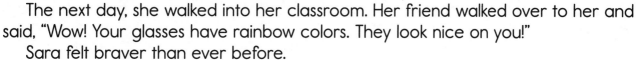

When Sara was a baby, she could see very well. As she grew older, Sara began to lose her eyesight. She could not see the board at school. This made her feel worried. When she felt nervous, she whispered, "I am happy. My eyes can see." This made her feel a little better.

Sara's eye doctor gave her strong glasses, but she still felt uneasy. She thought she looked silly in her glasses. Her mom said, "Sara, be brave and wear your glasses. You need them!"

Sara knew she needed the glasses. She decided she would not let anyone make her feel different or bully her.

The next day, she walked into her classroom. Her friend walked over to her and said, "Wow! Your glasses have rainbow colors. They look nice on you!"

Sara felt braver than ever before.

1. Who is the main character? _____

2. What is the message of the story? _____

3. How does Sara respond to her challenge? _____

4. What is the rhyme she whispers? _____

5. What happens at the end of the story? _____

Read the passage. Answer each question with a complete sentence.

Magnetism Is Everywhere

Electricity pulls two magnets together or pushes them apart. Electricity gives the magnets a **charge**, or force, that is either negative or positive. Many objects in space are **magnetic**. The center of Earth is magnetic and is made of iron. This special liquid gives Earth its magnetism. Where do we see magnetism on Earth? Look at a refrigerator. Magnets and other metal objects can stick to the door because they are charged. Also, a magnetic strip holds the refrigerator door closed.

6. What is the title of the passage? _____

7. What is the main idea?_____

8. Which two words are bold? _____

9. What does it mean when an object is magnetic?_____

10. Why did the author write the passage?_____

_____

11. Circle each short vowel word. Underline each long vowel word.

bike	boat	exit	fun	next
night	pail	rake	run	teeth

Read the passage.

Every October, Mrs. Lee's class goes on a field trip to the pumpkin farm. They walk around the barnyard and through the barn. They see some farm animals. Then, they go for a hayride. A big tractor pulls a large cart of hay. On the hayride, they ride through the apple orchard where people are picking apples. Later, they make applesauce. After the hayride, they go to the pumpkin patch. There are hundreds of pumpkins! Each student chooses a pumpkin to take home. It is always one of the most fun days of the year.

12. Answer each question with a complete sentence.

A. What is the main idea? _____

B. When is the class field trip?_____

C. Where do the students go on the hayride?_____

13. Circle each prefix. Underline each suffix.

careless   exit   hopeful   mistake   retell   subway   unhappy

14. Write an opinion sentence about the picture.

_____

_____

15. Circle the five linking words, also known as conjunctions.

a   also   and   because   but   or   the

16. Explain how to make a sandwich.
   A. First, _____

   B. Then, _____

   C. Next, _____

   D. Finally, _____

17. Write a complete sentence about an event that happened at school.

_____

_____

18. Write a complete sentence that tells your feelings about the event.

_____

_____

19. What do you look for when you revise and edit your writing? Check off each item.

When I revise and edit my writing, I . . .	Check ✔
look for spelling mistakes to correct.	
make sure I have ending punctuation.	
read my writing, and I do not make corrections.	
check if I have complete sentences.	

20. Write the plural form of each noun.

child _____

foot _____

mouse _____

21. Write an adjective to complete each sentence.

My _____ friend bought me an ice-cream cone.

We made a _____ dinner for Mom.

22. Place an apostrophe in each word to show ownership.

Paiges   Marys   Harrisons   Mr. Clarks   Justins

23. Write the holiday names with capital letters to show they are proper nouns.

thanksgiving   chinese new year   labor day

_____   _____   _____

24. Read the sentence.

My mom sighed as she pulled the *spare* tire out of the trunk of the car.

What does *spare* mean, based on the words you read?

_____

_____

After you review your student's diagnostic test, match those problems answered incorrectly to the Common Core State Standards below. Pay special attention to the pages that fall into these problem sections, and ensure that your student receives supervision in these areas. In this way, your student will strengthen these skills.

Answer Key: 1. Sara; 2. You can always choose to be positive about things. 3. She would not let anyone make her feel different. 4. I am happy. My eyes can see. 5. Sara receives a compliment. 6. Magnetism Is Everywhere; 7. Electricity is the driving force behind magnetism. 8. charge, magnetic; 9. When an object is magnetic, it can have an electric charge. 10. The author wants to inform the reader about magnetism. 11. short vowels: exit, fun, next, run; long vowels: bike, boat, night, pail, rake, teeth; 12. A. The class goes on a field trip to the pumpkin farm. B. October; C. through the apple orchard; 13. prefixes: *ex-*, *mis-*, *re-*, *sub-*, *un-*; suffixes: *-less*, *-ful*; 14. Answers will vary but sentence should have a subject, a verb, and adjectives. 15. also, and, because, but, or; 16. Answers will vary. 17. Answers will vary. 18. Answers will vary. 19. Answers will vary. 20. children, feet, mice; 21. Answers will vary. 22. Paige's, Mary's, Harrison's, Mr. Clark's, Justin's; 23. Thanksgiving, Chinese New Year, Labor Day; 24. *Spare* means "extra."

Common Core State Standards*		Test Item(s)	Practice Page(s)
Reading Standards for Literature			
Key Ideas and Details	2.RL.1 – 2.RL.3	1–3	13, 14, 16, 17
Craft and Structure	2.RL.4 – 2.RL.6	4, 5	18–21
Integration of Knowledge and Ideas	2.RL.7, 2.RL.9	3	22, 24
Range of Reading and Level of Text Complexity	2.RL.10	1	12, 15, 23, 25, 26
Reading Standards for Informational Text			
Key Ideas and Details	2.RI.1 – 2.RI.3	6–10	27–29, 40
Craft and Structure	2.RI.4 – 2.RI.6	6, 8–10	30–33, 35
Integration of Knowledge and Ideas	2.RI.7 – 2.RI.9	10	35–39, 41
Range of Reading and Level of Text Complexity	2.RI.10	6–10	27, 28, 30, 34, 36, 37, 40, 41, 53, 58
Reading Standards: Foundational Skills			
Phonics and Word Recognition	2.RF.3	11, 13	16, 42–50
Fluency	2.RF.4	12	21, 51, 52, 54
Writing			
Text Types and Purposes	2.W.1 – 2.W.3	14–18	55–57, 59, 65–67
Production and Distribution of Writing	2.W.4 – 2.W.6	19	60–64, 67, 68
Language			
Conventions of Standard English	2.L.1 – 2.L.2	20–23	13, 31, 54, 56, 57, 59, 71, 73–82, 90
Knowledge of Language	2.L.3	12	19, 65, 66
Vocabulary Acquisition and Use	2.L.4 – 2.L.6	24	26, 48, 83–90

* © Copyright 2010. National Governors Association Center for Best Practices and Council of Chief State School Officers. All rights reserved.

Read the story.

The Ants and the Cookie

One day, two ants went exploring. They came across two giant cookies. "These cookies are huge!" said the first ant.

"One of these cookies would feed my whole family for a month," said the second ant. "But, how can little ants like us carry such big cookies like these?"

"It seems impossible!" said the first ant. "But, I must try."

So, the first ant started to tug and pull at one cookie. Suddenly, a tiny piece broke off.

"I am going to take this piece back to my family," said the first ant.

"You go ahead," said the second ant. "I'm not going to waste my time on such a small piece of cookie. I will find a way to take the whole cookie back to my family."

So, the first ant went home with her small piece of cookie. Soon, the first ant returned. She found the second ant still pushing and shoving the other cookie, but he was unable to move it. Again, the first ant broke off a small piece of cookie and took it back home. This went on for most of the day. The first ant kept carrying small pieces of cookie back to her family until she had moved the entire cookie. The second ant finally tired of trying to complete a task that seemed too big to do. She went home with nothing.

❑ **I can read various texts with ease and understanding.**

Answer the questions.

1. How did the first ant carry the cookie home?
   A. She dragged it.
   B. She carried a little bit at a time.
   C. She ate most of it first.

2. What happened to the second ant?
   A. She got tired of trying and quit.
   B. She carried the cookie home.
   C. She ate the cookie.

Write the past tense of each verb (action word).

3. come _____

4. say _____

5. feed _____

6. take _____

7. go _____

8. break _____

9. keep _____

10. bite _____

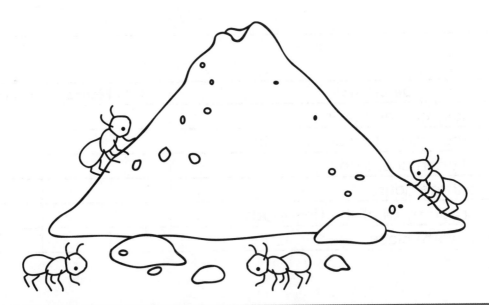

❑ **I can ask and answer questions about a text.**
❑ **I can form and use the past tense of most irregular verbs.**

Read the story. Identify the lesson, or moral, of the story. Then, read each description. Decide if it describes the City Mouse, the Country Mouse, or both mice. Write an X in the correct box.

City Mouse, Country Mouse

Once upon a time, a city mouse went to visit her friend in the country. The country mouse had spent the day gathering grain and dried pieces of corn to greet her friend with a nice meal. The city mouse was surprised to find her poor friend living in a cold tree stump and eating such scraps. So, she invited the country mouse to visit her in the city. The country mouse agreed.

The country mouse could not believe her eyes when she arrived! Her friend lived in a warm hole behind the fireplace of a large home. She was even surprised to find all of the fine foods that were left behind after a party the night before. The country mouse wished that she could live in the city as well.

Suddenly, the family's cat ran in and chased the two mice away. He nearly caught the country mouse with his sharp claws. As the friends raced back to the mouse hole, the country mouse said, "I'm sorry, friend, but I would rather live a simple life eating grain and corn than live a fancy life in fear!" The country mouse went back home.

1. What is the moral of the story? _____

_____

_____

Description	City Mouse	Country Mouse
She feasted daily on fine foods.		
She would rather have a simple, safe life.		
She gathered grain and corn.		
She lived in a large house.		
She was surprised by all of the fine foods.		
She lived in a warm place.		

❑ **I can retell stories with understanding.**

A **fable** is a story with a lesson, or moral. This story is an example of a fable. Read the story and answer the questions.

The Mouse and His Food

One day, a little mouse sat inside his little house inside a log. "Oh, dear," the mouse said. "I have nothing to eat but this small seed. Surely, I will go hungry." So, the little mouse set out to find some food.

Soon, the little mouse found two acorns. He took the acorns to his house. "Oh, dear," the mouse said. "I have nothing to eat but these two acorns and a small seed. What if the rains come and wash them away? Surely, I will go hungry." So, the mouse set out to find more food.

Soon, he found a corncob. He took the corncob back to his house. "Oh, dear," the mouse said. "I have nothing to eat but these two acorns, a small seed, and this corncob. What if the winds come and blow them away? Surely, I will go hungry." So, the mouse set out to find more food.

Soon, he found six walnuts. He took the walnuts back to his house. "Oh, dear," the mouse said. "I have nothing to eat but these two acorns, a small seed, this corncob, and these six walnuts. What if the snow comes and freezes them all? Surely, I will go hungry." So, the mouse set out to find more food.

This went on for days. Finally, the mouse gathered more food than 10 mice could eat in a year. Soon, the rains, the winds, and the snow did come. But, none of the food washed away. None of the food blew away. And, none of the food froze. But, because the mouse could not eat all of the food, the food rotted. Because the mouse could not eat rotten food, he went hungry.

❏ **I can read various texts with ease and understanding.**

Circle the correct answer.

1. What is the lesson, or moral, of the story?
   A. Weather can ruin your plans.
   B. Storing more than you need may cause problems.
   C. Do not be too fearful of the future.

2. What word best describes the mouse?
   A. friendly
   B. hungry
   C. fearful

3. What is the mouse afraid of?
   A. starving
   B. being eaten by a cat
   C. being washed away by the rain

4. What happened to the mouse's food?
   A. It blew away.
   B. It rotted.
   C. The mouse ate it.

5. What happened to the mouse?
   A. He went hungry.
   B. He had enough food to eat.
   C. He shared the food that he gathered.

Homophones are words that sound the same but have different meanings and spellings. Find the homophone in the fable for each word.

6. won _____

7. deer _____

8. sum _____

9. too _____

10. daze _____

❑ I can retell stories with understanding.
❑ I can read words that are spelled irregularly.

Characters respond to major events and challenges in a story.
They show action and emotion when they respond to events.

Read the story. Answer each question with a complete sentence.

No Broken Friendship

Matthew and Brandon have been best friends since kindergarten. One day, when Brandon was playing at Matthew's house, Brandon jumped from the swing set and landed in a strange way. "My arm!" he shouted. One look at Brandon's arm told Matthew that it was broken.

Brandon's parents took him to the hospital where the doctor took an X-ray of his arm. The doctor put a blue cast on his arm and told Brandon that his bones would grow back in place. He also reminded Brandon not to take any risks, such as playing too roughly, during the next eight weeks.

The next day, Brandon took his X-ray to school and told the class his story. They had many questions, and Brandon answered them as best as he could. Matthew asked, "Do you want to play tic-tac-toe instead of wall ball at recess today?"

"Great idea!" Brandon answered.

1. How did Brandon respond to his mishap? _____

_____

_____

2. How did the doctor respond? _____

_____

_____

3. How did Matthew respond? _____

_____

_____

❑ **I can understand events and challenges in a story.**

This poem has the rhythm of a swing going back and forth. Read the poem aloud to someone. Try to read it with the rhythm of a swing.

The Swing

How do you like to go up in a swing,
Up in the air so blue?
Oh, I do think it is the pleasantest thing
Ever a child could do!

Up in the air and over the wall,
Till I can see so wide,
Rivers and trees and cattle and all
Over the countryside—

Till I look down on the garden green,
Down on the roof so brown—
Up in the air I go flying again,
Up in the air and down!

Robert Louis Stevenson

❑ **I can read poetry with rhythm.**

Prepositions are words, such as *up* and *down*, that tell position. Circle the preposition in each sentence.

1. The balloon sailed into the clouds.

2. The ball landed on the roof.

3. The girl jumped over the wall.

4. The boy ran down the stairs.

5. The dog is in the house.

The suffix *-est* means "most." Rewrite each word with the *-est* suffix.

6. hard _____

7. long_____

8. green _____

9. fresh _____

10. deep_____

11. small _____

12. kind _____

13. fast_____

14. slow _____

15. high_____

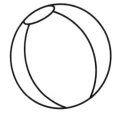

❑ **I can describe how words have meaning.**
❑ **I can use what I have learned about good language.**

Read the story aloud with a partner. Answer each question with a complete sentence.

The Gift

"Happy Mother's Day," Nathan said. Nathan gave his mom a large box with a pretty bow.

"What is it?" his mother asked.

"You have to guess," Nathan said. "I'll give you a hint. It's soft and blue."

"Can I wear it?" his mother asked.

"Yes," Nathan said.

"I think I know," his mother said. She opened the box. "Thank you! It is just what I wanted," she said.

Nathan's mom took the gift out of the box. She put it on over her head. She put her arms in the sleeves. It fit just right. Nathan's mother gave him a big hug.

1. How does the story begin?_____

_____

2. How does the story end?_____

_____

3. Who said, "It is just what I wanted"? _____

_____

4. Who said, "I'll give you a hint"?_____

_____

❑ **I can describes the events of a story and their purposes.**
❑ **I can show how characters have different points of view.**

> A **skit** is a short play. It is a dialogue between characters.

Read the skit aloud with a partner. Read the words in quotes. Perform the words in italics.

Snow Fun

Joshua: "I think I see snowflakes!"
Manuel: (*surprised*)"Really? Let me take a look."
     (*Manuel walks to the window.*)
Joshua: "Do you see them? They are really falling now!"
Manuel: "You are right. The snow makes me want to play outside!"
Joshua: (*smiles*) "I think we should get dressed and build something."
Manuel: "What should we build? A snowman?"
Joshua: "I know something better that we can build!"
Manuel: "What is it?"
Joshua: (*excited*) "Let's build a snow fort!"

Answer the questions.

1. Who prefers to build a snowman?_____

2. Who prefers to build a snow fort?_____

☐ **I can show how characters have different points of view.**
☐ **I can read with purpose and understanding.**

The **setting** is the place and time in which a story takes place. As a story unfolds, the setting may change. The setting gives the reader information about where the story happens.

Read the text. Then, use the information given to draw the settings that are described.

In the fight to save his tribe's land, Chief Seattle spoke of his desire to preserve the American land. In the book *Brother Eagle, Sister Sky* by Susan Jeffers (Puffin, 2002), Chief Seattle begs us to care for Earth as we would our mothers. He also questions what will become of all people if we do not.

If people use the land wisely, Earth will always have beautiful forests, oceans, and deserts full of living plants and animals.

If our land becomes too polluted, we will lose natural beauty. Factories and electrical wires will replace the forests, oceans, and deserts.

☐ **I can use pictures and words to figure out the parts of a story.**

People from many cultures write stories in different languages but with similar themes. Read the stories from two different cultures. Then, answer the questions.

Cinderella

Once upon a time, there was a girl named Cinderella who lived with her mean stepmother and two evil stepsisters. The three women made Cinderella do all of the chores, and she was not allowed to leave the house.

A royal ball was planned, and all of the women in the town were invited to meet the prince. Cinderella's stepmother locked her in a room so that she could not go to the ball. Cinderella's animal friends found the key and unlocked the door. But, Cinderella did not have a dress to wear. She ran outside and cried.

A fairy godmother appeared. She magically gave Cinderella a dress and glass slippers. Cinderella looked beautiful! She rode to the ball in a carriage but could only stay until midnight. When she arrived, she was able to dance with the prince. Time went by quickly, and Cinderella had to leave. At midnight, her dress turned to rags! She ran and left a glass slipper on the stairs. The prince found it and kept it.

The prince's father, the king, sent his squire to every home in the town. He needed to find the woman whose foot fit into the slipper. He came to Cinderella's house, but Cinderella's stepmother had locked her in a room. Thankfully, her animal friends helped her again. Cinderella ran downstairs to the squire and tried on the shoe. It fit, and she left to meet the prince. They lived happily ever after.

□ **I can read various texts with ease and understanding.**

Yeh-Shen

There once was a girl named Yeh-Shen who was raised by her mean stepmother. As Yeh-Shen grew older, her stepmother made her do chores. The other daughters did not have to do any work, but Yeh-Shen did.

There was a festival in town, and Yeh-Shen wanted to go. It was a special gathering where young people had fun. Yeh-Shen's stepmother and her daughters went to the festival. They told Yeh-Shen she had to stay home. Yeh-Shen secretly went to the festival after she used magic fish bones. The bones gave her a beautiful feathered dress and golden slippers. At the festival, the king saw Yeh-Shen. As he moved toward her, Yeh-Shen had to run. Her stepmother was nearby! She left behind a golden slipper, and the king picked it up.

The king ordered his soldiers to search the kingdom for the mysterious woman with the golden slipper. Many women tried on the slipper, but no one could fit in the tiny shoe. Yeh-Shen went to the king's pavilion in the night and asked to try on the slipper. It fit perfectly. The king soon married Yeh-Shen.

1. How are Yeh-Shen and Cinderella similar? Write two complete sentences.

_____

_____

_____

2. How are Yeh-Shen and Cinderella different? Write two complete sentences.

_____

_____

_____

❏ **I can compare and contrast characters in different versions of the same story.**

Read the poem.

Animal Dreams

I wonder if animals have dreams.

Does a fish dream of swimming in the sky?
Does a bird dream of flying in the ocean?

I wonder if monkeys dream of learning in school,
While children dream of swinging from vines.

Or, maybe worms dream of being as big as snakes,
And snakes dream of having legs like a centipede.

I wonder.

☐ **I can read various texts with ease and understanding.**

Use the poem on page 25 to answer the questions.

1. What does the author wonder about?
   A. if monkeys wish they could go to school
   B. if animals have dreams
   C. if animals are happy

Write *T* for each statement that is true. Write *F* for each statement that is false.

2. _____ Fish swim in the sky.

3. _____ Monkeys swing from vines.

4. _____ Snakes have legs like centipedes.

Write the root word of each word.

5. swimming _____

6. flying _____

7. learning_____

8. swinging _____

9. being _____

10. having _____

❑ **I can read various texts with ease and understanding.**
❑ **I can use a word I know to figure out the meaning of another word.**

Read the passage. Answer each question with a complete sentence.

Night Navigators

Many people do not realize what bats do for us. Bats are some of our best nighttime insect exterminators. More than 850 kinds of bats exist in the world. Bats can be anywhere from 1.5 inches (1.3 cm) long to more than 15 inches (38 cm) long. Although most bats eat just insects, some dine on fruit and the nectar of flowers. As the only flying mammal on Earth, bats should be recognized for their contributions to people.

Aside from controlling the insect population, bats are the main pollinators and seed spreaders for many tropical trees such as mango, guava, cashew, clove, and Brazil nut. Bats use their sonar-guided ears and mouths to enjoy a nightly dinner of millions of mosquitoes, mayflies, and moths.

1. How many different kinds of bats are in the world? _____

_____

2. What do bats like to eat?_____

_____

3. How long can some species of bats be?_____

_____

4. What kinds of tropical trees depend on the bat for spreading their seeds? _____

_____

5. What helps bats find mosquitoes, mayflies, and moths?_____

_____

☐ I can ask and answer questions about the text to show my understanding.
☐ I can read and understand informational texts.

Main ideas of different passages can be connected because they share things in common.

Read the passage and answer the questions.

Chemicals are everywhere. They make up the air, our homes, our food, and even our bodies. Chemicals help make things different from each other. They make apples sweet and lemons sour. They make leaves green.

When chemicals mix to form something new, it is called a reaction. As a banana ripens, it turns from green to yellow. This is from chemicals changing. When you roast a marshmallow, you are watching chemicals change in a tasty way!

1. What would be a good title for the passage?
   A. Chemicals in Our Bodies
   B. Chemicals Are Tasty
   C. Chemicals Around Us

2. What is the main idea of the first paragraph?
   A. Apples are sweet.
   B. Chemicals are everywhere.
   C. Leaves are green.

3. What is the main idea of the second paragraph?
   A. Chemicals can mix to form something new.
   B. Bananas turn from green to yellow.
   C. Chocolate milk is tasty.

☐ I can tell the topic and focus of one or more paragraphs.
☐ I can read and understand informational texts.

Main ideas of different passages can be connected because they share things in common.

Read each passage. Circle the letter of the answer that tells the main idea. Then, identify the connection between the passages.

1. George Washington grew up in Virginia. He liked to play games outside. He also helped his family on their farm. When he was seven, he started school.

A. George Washington was the first president.
B. George Washington grew up in Virginia.
C. George Washington went to school.

2. Abraham Lincoln had many different jobs. He worked as a farmer and a carpenter. He also helped on riverboats. He worked in a store. Later, he became a lawyer.

A. Abraham Lincoln was born in a log cabin.
B. Abraham Lincoln liked to read books.
C. Abraham Lincoln had many different jobs.

3. Martin Luther King, Jr., won the Nobel Peace Prize. This prize is given to a person who has worked hard for peace. The prize is money. Martin gave the money to people who helped him work for peace.

A. Martin Luther King, Jr., won the Nobel Peace Prize.
B. Martin Luther King, Jr., believed all people were born equal.
C. We celebrate Martin Luther King Day in January.

4. What do all of the passages have in common? Write a complete sentence.

_____

_____

_____

☐ **I can describe how details in the text are connected.**

Read the passage. Focus on the bold words and think about their meanings.
Underline important information.

The Koala

Koalas live in Australia. They spend most of their time high up in tall **eucalyptus** trees. Koalas eat the leaves from the trees. They eat about 2 to 3 pounds (0.9 to 1.4 kg) of leaves every day. Koalas drink very little water. The eucalyptus leaves give koalas the water they need.

Many people think koalas are bears because they look like bear cubs. Koalas are not bears. They are **marsupials**. Marsupials are a special kind of mammal. They have pouches to keep their babies warm and safe.

Koalas have pouches just like another animal whose name begins with the letter *K*. Can you guess what the animal is? It is a kangaroo.

☐ I can determine the meaning of words in a second-grade text.

Use the passage on page 30 to answer the questions.

1 . What is the passage about?
    A. Australia
    B. koalas
    C. eucalyptus trees

2 . Where do koalas spend most of their time?
    A. in eucalyptus trees
    B. in their mothers' pouches
    C. in caves with bears

3 . What is a *marsupial*?
    A. a mammal with a pouch
    B. an animal that swims underwater
    C. a mammal with a long trunk

4 . What is *eucalyptus*?
    A. a type of marsupial
    B. a type of tree
    C. a baby koala

Write the plural of each word.

5. koala   _____

6. marsupial   _____

7. pouch   _____

8. baby   _____

9. leaf   _____

☐ **I can determine the meanings of words in a text.**

A story either can be true or pretend. The sentences in a story tell you what the story is about. The title helps tell you what the story is mostly about.

Read each story. Then, match each title to the correct story.

A. The Turtle Dream	B. The Sleepover
C. A New Puppy	D. A Wish Before Bed

1.	2.
Sally made a wish every night before going to sleep. She would look into the sky for the brightest star. Then, she would close her eyes and make a wish.	Sally fell asleep in the car on the way to the zoo. She dreamed that she was a flying turtle. She flew all around the zoo. No one could catch her.
3.	**4.**
Sally had her friend Jill sleep over. They watched a video and ate popcorn. They made a tent out of blankets. They slept in the tent.	Sally woke up early. She was excited. Today, her family was getting a puppy. They had already named the puppy Muffett.

☐ **I know how to use text features to find information.**

As you read, you will notice the author is writing for a purpose. In the passage, the author describes similarities and differences. They will help you draw conclusions or make decisions.

Read the passage and answer the questions.

Cars Then and Now

Have you ever been in a convertible car? If you had lived long ago when Henry Ford started making cars, you may have owned a convertible. Henry Ford built all kinds of cars. He built the first cars that were low enough in price for many people to buy them. The cars could not go as fast as the cars today, but they looked like a lot of fun!

Henry Ford's cars were different from the cars that you see today. The cars used gas, but the tanks were under the drivers' seats. People had to lift the seats to put gas in the cars. Sometimes, the cars would not start in the cold weather unless people poured hot water under the hoods. Many of the cars did not have bumpers or mirrors because those things cost extra money. Still, they were a great way to get around, just as our cars are today.

1. What is the author's purpose?_____

_____

2. Would you rather have a car from the past or a car from today? Make a list of similarities and differences to help you decide.

How Cars of the Past and Cars of Today Are Similar

A. _____

B. _____

How Cars of the Past and Cars of Today Are Different

A. _____

B. _____

☐ **I can tell the main purpose of a text.**

Read the story.

Twins

Chris and William are twins. They are brothers who were born on December 22. Twins that look almost exactly alike are called identical twins. Chris and William are fraternal twins. That means they do not look exactly alike. Identical and fraternal twins are born on the same day.

William has curly red hair. Chris has straight brown hair. Chris's eyes are green. William's eyes are blue. Another difference between them is their teeth. Chris is missing his two front teeth. William has all of his teeth, and he has braces.

Both boys like to play baseball. Sometimes, they play third base. Sometimes, they play catcher. Both of them can throw the ball well. It can be fun to have a twin.

❑ **I can read and understand informational texts.**

Use the story on page 34 to answer the questions.

1. What is the main idea of the story?
    A. Chris and William are fraternal twins.
    B. Chris and William have different teachers.
    C. Chris and William do not look exactly alike.

2. What are the two types of twins? _____

3. What does the word *identical* mean? _____

4. What does the word *fraternal* mean?_____

5. Read each description. Decide if it describes Chris, William, or both brothers. Write an X in the correct box.

Description	Chris	William
born on December 22		
curly red hair and blue eyes		
straight brown hair and green eyes		
missing two front teeth		
good ball player		

☐ I can use images to help me understand a text.
☐ I can figure out the meaning of words in a text.

Read the passage. Answer each question with a complete sentence.

Germs

Germs are things we do not want to share. Germs can make people sick. Even though we cannot see germs, they get into the body in many ways. Germs can get into the body through the nose, mouth, eyes, and cuts in the skin. We share germs when we drink from the same cups or eat off of the same plates.

Here are some helpful tips to keep germs to yourself and to stay healthy:

- Wash your hands with soap.
- Cover your mouth when you
- cough or sneeze.
- Do not share food or drinks.
- Keep your fingers out of your nose and mouth.
- Do not rub your eyes.
- Get a little bit of sunshine and fresh air.
- Eat healthful meals.
- Get plenty of sleep.

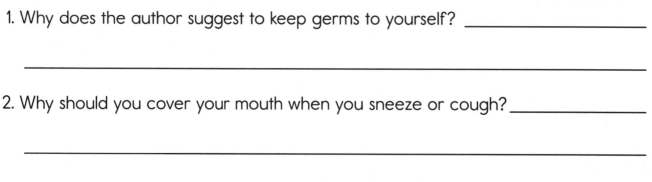

1. Why does the author suggest to keep germs to yourself? _____

_____

2. Why should you cover your mouth when you sneeze or cough?_____

_____

☐ I can understand reasons that support the author's text.
☐ I can read and understand informational texts.

Read each text about safety. Think about how they are the same and different.

Wearing a helmet is important when riding a bike. Boys and girls ride bikes on grass and on sidewalks. The different types of ground can be tricky when riding. Animal holes are hidden in the grass. Rocks and sand are on sidewalks. By wearing helmets, boys and girls keep their heads safe.

Gardening gloves are useful. They protect our hands and wrists from pesky prickles. Rose bushes can have many sharp thorns. Gloves also keep hands safe from sunburn while outdoors in a sunny garden. The gloves even keep hands clean. Gardens are full of moist soil. The dirt can get under nails and in between fingers. Gardening gloves are very handy!

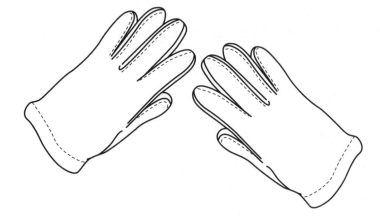

☐ I can compare and contrast two texts about the same topic.
☐ I can read and understand informational texts.

Use the texts on page 37 to answer the questions. Write in complete sentences.

1. Why is it safe to wear a helmet when riding a bike?_____

_____

2. Why is it safe to wear gloves when gardening? _____

_____

3. How are the two texts alike?_____

_____

4. How are the two texts different? _____

_____

Draw lines to connect the **verbs,** or action words, with the related verbs.

5. toss   grab

6. clutch   close

7. slam   throw

Draw lines to connect the **adjectives,** or describing words, with the related adjectives.

8. thin   tiny

9. small   gigantic

10. large   slender

☐ I can compare and contrast two texts on the same topic.
☐ I can tell the difference between synonyms.

Charts and tables are helpful for organizing information. To read a chart, match the given information from the top and the side to find new information in the boxes.

Use the chart to answer the questions.

	Monday	Tuesday	Wednesday	Thursday	Friday
Reading	Unit 1	Unit 2	Unit 3	Unit 4	Unit 5
Writing	brainstorming ideas	rough draft	revised writing	edited writing	final draft
Math	pp. 21–22	pp. 23–24	pp. 25–26	pp. 27–30	line graph
Science	plant seeds		recording sheet		recording sheet
Social Studies		map		time line	

1. What assignment is due on Wednesday in science? _____

2. What assignment is due on Thursday in writing? _____

3. On what day is the time line due in social studies? _____

4. In what subject do we read pages 23–24 on Tuesday? _____

5. What assignment is due on Monday in social studies? _____

6. On what day is Unit 3 due in reading? _____

7. On what day is the line graph due in math?_____

8. What assignment is due Tuesday in writing?_____

❑ I can use diagrams to understand text.

Name_____

The **sequence** of a story can be imagined as you read it. Watch for key words to help you remember the order of important events.

Read the passage. Then, put the events in the correct sequence.

The Midnight Ride

Early on April 19, 1775, Paul Revere and many other colonists were ready to fight against the British army. They called themselves minutemen because they had to be ready to fight at a minute's notice. First, Paul waited for a signal from American spies. They knew the British would eventually move toward Lexington and Concord, but they were unsure whether the British would travel by land or across the water. When Paul received word, he would signal the other minutemen, telling them from which direction the British were coming. Next, he would ride his horse quickly through the area, shouting the news that the British were coming.

At last, the word came from the spies. Paul immediately ordered two lanterns to be hung in the tall tower of the church, a signal that the British were coming by boat. Then, he mounted his horse and rode fast into the night. Paul knew the importance of warning the minutemen to prepare. The British army had more men and defense, so the minutemen would have to surprise them. Paul rode through Lexington, shouting the news. But, as he rode out of town, a British soldier caught him. Meanwhile, two other riders made it farther and told the minutemen to be ready in Concord.

Soon, the British army reached Concord. They were surprised by the minutemen and fled the area. The minutemen that were awakened had won their first fight, and someday there would be freedom.

Number the sentences from 1 to 6 to put the events in the correct sequence.

_____ A British soldier caught Paul Revere.

_____ Two lanterns were lit in the church tower.

_____ The minutemen surprised the British army.

_____ Paul Revere rode through Lexington.

_____ Paul Revere received word from the spies.

_____ Two other riders warned the minutemen to gather in Concord.

☐ **I can describe how details in the text are connected.**
☐ **I can read and understand informational texts.**

Use the schedule to answer the questions.

		Times							
		7:00	7:30	8:00	8:30	9:00	9:30	10:00	10:30
Channels	**2**	Quiz Game Show	Jump Start		Summer the Dog			News	
	4	Lucky Guess	You Should Know	Wednesday Night at the Movies *Friends Forever*				News	
	5	Best Friends	Mary's Secret	Where They Are	Time to Hope	Tom's Talk Show		News	
	7	123 Oak Street	Lost Alone	One More Time	Sports			News	
	11	Your Health	Eating Right	Food News		Cooking with Kate		Home Décor	Shop Now
	24	Silly Rabbit	Clyde the Clown	Balls o' Fun	Slime and Rhyme	Cartoon Alley		Fun Times	Make Me Laugh

1. What does the schedule show?
   A. times and channels of TV shows
   B. times and channels of radio shows
   C. the number of people who like different shows

2. On what channels can you watch news at 10:00?
   A. 2, 5, and 11
   B. 3, 4, and 11
   C. 2, 4, 5, and 7

3. What time is the show "Silly Rabbit" on?
   A. 7:00
   B. 7:30
   C. 8:30

☐ **I can tell how a picture helps explain something in the text.**
☐ **I can read and understand informational texts.**

Name_____

Consonant blends are two or more consonants next to each other at the beginning or the end of a word. Each letter makes its own sound.

Examples: *str* in <u>str</u>aw, *gl* in <u>gl</u>ass, *ld* in o<u>ld</u>, *nt* in be<u>nt</u>, *ft* in le<u>ft</u>

Consonant digraphs are two consonants next to each other at the beginning or the end of a word that usually make one sound.

Examples: *sh* in <u>sh</u>ip, *th* in ba<u>th</u>, *ch* in <u>ch</u>ildren

Write the correct consonant blend or digraph to complete the word in each sentence.

1. A wi____ ____ is one of the movable, feathered appendages a bird uses to fly.

2. A ba____ ____ is a place to put money.

3. Sa____ ____ is often found at a beach.

4. If you sco____ ____ someone, you discipline or correct her.

5. Ceme____ ____ is a hard material used in sidewalks and building construction.

6. Cou____ ____ is a synonym for *sofa*.

7. A tre____ ____ is a fad in clothing, toys, or other markets.

8. Twelve mon____ ____s are in a year.

9. If you spri ____ ____, you run a short distance.

10. The lu____ ____s are part of the human respiratory system that help take in oxygen.

11. Pi____ ____ is the color of bubble gum, piglets, and some flowers.

12. Acorn, spaghetti, and butternut are types of squa____ ____.

❏ **I can use phonics skills.**
❏ **I can use word study and phonics skills to read words.**

© Carson-Dellosa • CD-104609

42

There are five main vowels: *a, e, i, o,* and *u.* The **short vowel sounds** are *a* as in c*a*t, *e* as in b*e*d, *i* as in sh*i*p, *o* as in b*o*x, and *u* as in t*u*b.

Complete each word with the correct short vowel sound.

 1. c ____ p

 2. d ____ t

 3. l ____ g

 4. f ____ n

 5. m ____ p

 6. l ____ ps

 7. p ____ g

 8. n ____ t

 9. h ____ t

 10. tr ____ ck

Cut out the letters. Glue them to make three short vowel words.

☐ **I can understand short vowel sounds.**

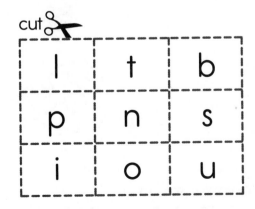

cut

l	t	b
p	n	s
i	o	u

Name_____

When a letter sounds like its name, it makes a **long vowel sound**.

Examples: *a* as in *t_a_ke, i* as in *l_i_ke*

When a word has a consonant-vowel-consonant-*e* pattern (CVCe), the vowel sound is usually long, and the *e* is silent.

Examples: *name, ride, note, cute*

Complete each word with the correct long vowel sound and a silent e.

 1. c ____ p ____

 2. c ____ k ____

 3. br ____ d ____

4. airpl ____ n ____

 5. b ____ n ____

 6. k ____ t ____

 7. r ____ k ____

 8. p ____ p ____

 9. m ____ l ____

 10. c ____ n ____

 11. c ____ n ____

 12. t ____ p ____

❑ **I can understand long vowel sounds.**

44

> **Vowel digraphs** are two vowels next to each other that usually make one sound. The vowel digraphs *ai*, *ea*, *ee*, and *oa* often make a long vowel sound.
>
> Examples: w<u>ai</u>t, r<u>ea</u>l, b<u>ee</u>, g<u>oa</u>t

Read each clue. Complete each word with the correct vowel digraph.

1. You do this when you are tired.

   sl _____ _____ p

2. This is water that falls from the sky.

   r _____ _____ n

3. You use this in the bath.

   s _____ _____ p

4. Jack carried this up a hill.

   p _____ _____ l

5. You ride in this on the water.

   b _____ _____ t

6. You play in the sand there.

   b _____ _____ ch

7. You do this with your eyes.

   s _____ _____

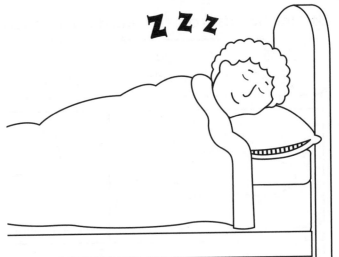

☐ **I know the spellings and sounds of common vowel pairs.**

Name_____

These letter combinations also make special sounds.

ou mouse	ow flower	oi coin	oy boy	ew news 

Use the words from the word bank to label the pictures.

boil	chew	cloud	crown	growl	house
jewel	mouth	point	screw	soil	tower

1. _____	2. _____	3. _____
4. _____	5. _____	6. _____
7. _____	8. _____	9. _____
10. _____	11. _____	12. _____

❏ **I know the spellings and sounds of common vowel pairs.**

All words have parts called **syllables**. The number of syllables in a word is the same as the number of vowel sounds you hear in the word.

Examples: *nine* = one syllable and one vowel sound
zebra = two syllables and two vowel sounds

Complete the table.

Words	Syllables	Vowel Sounds	Words	Syllables	Vowel Sounds
1. apron	2	2	6. playful		
2. three			7. lady		
3. nail			8. favorite		
4. window			9. grape		
5. relaxing			10. sweet		

Sort the words above by the number of syllables.

1	2	3

☐ **I can understand long vowel sounds.**
☐ **I can read two-syllable words with long vowels.**

A **prefix** is a part of a word. It is at the beginning of many words. It is a syllable. Add one prefix from the word bank to each word below. Write a definition for the new word.

ex- (out)	re- (again)	sub- (under)	un- (not)

1. _____marine: _____

2. _____it: _____

3. _____do: _____

4. _____view: _____

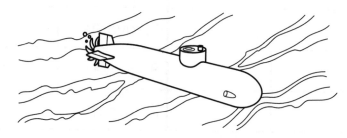

A **suffix** is a part of a word. It is at the end of many words. It can be a syllable. Add one suffix from the word bank to each word below. Write a definition for the new word.

-er (one who)	-en (made of)	-ful (full of)	-less (without)

5. play_____: _____

6. hope_____: _____

7. work_____: _____

8. wood_____: _____

☐ I can read and write words with common prefixes and suffixes.
☐ I can determine the meaning of a new word when a prefix or suffix has been added.

When *r* follows most vowels, it takes control, and the vowel makes a new sound.

Examples: f<u>ar</u>, h<u>er</u>, s<u>ir</u>, f<u>ur</u>

Write the word from the word bank that best completes each sentence.

after	bird	car	dark	first	fur	stars

1. We ride in the _____ to the zoo.

2. I want to be _____ in line.

3. We see many animals with _____.

4. The _____ has colorful feathers.

5. We will eat _____ the sea lion show.

6. It is _____ when we drive home.

7. I see many _____ in the sky.

❑ **I can name words that are spelled differently from how they sound.**

Homophones are two words that sound alike but are spelled differently and have different meanings.

Example: *tail, tale*

Write the correct homophone to complete each sentence.

1. I cannot believe you ate that _____ cake by yourself!
   (whole, hole)

2. Did you get a letter in the _____ today?
   (male, mail)

3. The _____ lives in a beautiful castle.
   (prints, prince)

4. _____ you help me with my homework?
   (Would, Wood)

5. My grandmother has a lovely _____ garden.
   (rose, rows)

6. I put my bike in the garage when it _____.
   (reigns, rains)

7. That tiger has large _____!
   (paws, pause)

8. You need two cups of _____ to make the cake.
   (flower, flour)

9. Comb your _____ before you go to school.
   (hare, hair)

10. That skunk has a strong _____!
    (cent, scent)

❑   **I can read words that are spelled irregularly.**

Name_____

Read each story. Answer each question with a complete sentence.

Maddie and her family went to the park for a picnic. They placed a red blanket on the ground. Maddie's mom set the picnic basket on the blanket. Then, they all went for a walk. When they returned, hundreds of ants were on the blanket. Maddie's dad grabbed the picnic basket. The family moved to a picnic table to enjoy their lunch.

1. What was the problem?_____

_____

2. How did Maddie's family solve the problem?_____

_____

Today was the big race at Jayden's school. Jayden was excited about the race. He was a fast runner. He ran the fastest when he wore his black tennis shoes. After breakfast, he went to his room to put on his black shoes. The shoes were not there. Where could they be? Jayden decided to ask everyone in his family if they had seen his shoes. He found his younger brother Michael wearing his shoes. Michael wanted to run fast too!

3. What was the problem?_____

_____

4. How did Jayden solve the problem?_____

_____

☐ **I can read fluently and understand a story.**

Read the first passage to a partner. Complete the checklist with your partner. Then, have your partner read the second passage to you. Complete the second checklist with your partner.

1. Raccoons have large appetites. They will eat just about anything! Raccoons will eat fruit, vegetables, fish, insects, and even garbage. They do most of their eating in the spring and summer months when plenty of food is around. This gives raccoons body fat for the winter.

Self-Check Questions	Yes	No
Did I read all of the words accurately and correctly?		
Did I read at the correct rate (not too fast, not too slow)?		
Did I read with feeling and expression?		

2. The American crocodile is an endangered species. Crocodiles like to live in rivers and swamps. The United States has laws to protect the crocodiles. Crocodiles are found in the waters of other countries too. Some of those places do not have laws to protect crocodiles.

Self-Check Questions	Yes	No
Did I read all of the words accurately and correctly?		
Did I read at the correct rate (not too fast, not too slow)?		
Did I read with feeling and expression?		

☐ I can read with purpose and understanding.
☐ I can read aloud with accuracy and expression.

Read the passage.

Changing with the Seasons

We are not the only living things to change how we protect our bodies with the seasons. We change our clothing with the seasons to protect us from the weather. Animals change their outer coverings to protect themselves when the seasons change. They know when it is time to change.

For example, the arctic fox has a thick, white fur coat in the winter. A white coat is not easy to see in the snow. This helps the fox hide from enemies. When spring comes, the fox's fur changes to brown. It is then the color of the ground.

A bird called the ptarmigan, or snow chicken, has white feathers in the winter. It is also hard to see in the snow. In the spring, the bird **molts**. This means that it sheds all of its feathers. The bird grows new feathers that are speckled. When the bird is very still, it looks like a rock.

Write an important fact from each paragraph. Reread as necessary.

1. _____

2. _____

3. _____

☐ I can use context clues to correct my reading.
☐ I can reread if necessary.
☐ I can read and understand informational text.

Use the passage on page 53 to answer the questions.

1. What is the passage mostly about?
   A. how people change with the seasons
   B. how seasons change
   C. how animals change with the seasons

2. What color is the arctic fox?
   A. brown
   B. white
   C. black

3. What happens to the ptarmigan in the spring?
   A. It molts.
   B. It flies south.
   C. Its feathers turn red.

4. What does *molts* mean?
   A. changes colors
   B. sheds feathers
   C. hides from an enemy

Make each sentence longer by adding details.

5. The baby ate. _____

_____

6. I watched. _____

_____

7. Erica ran. _____

_____

8. Darrell rode. _____

_____

☐ **I can read with purpose and understanding.**
☐ **I can expand sentences by adding details.**

A **fact** is something you know is true. An **opinion** is what you believe about something.

Read the passage. Then, write facts and opinions from the passage.

American Indian Dances

American Indians have long used dancing to express themselves. Each dance has a deep and emotional meaning to a given tribe. The Great Plains Indian dancers dress in feathers and painted masks for the fast and colorful Fancy Dance. It is the most exciting of the dances. Other Indian dancers perform the Hoop Dance with large hoops that they swing and shape to resemble patterns from nature. It is by far the most difficult dance. The Pueblo Indian dancers, wearing butterfly headdresses, imitate the peaceful life of the butterfly with the Butterfly Dance. The dance is graceful and beautiful.

Write three facts from the passage.

1. _____

2. _____

3. _____

Write three opinions from the passage.

4. _____

5. _____

6. _____

Write one opinion of your own about the passage.

7. _____

_____

❑ **I can write about a topic or a book and tell how I feel about it.**

Use your answers on page 55 to answer the questions.

1. Write an opinion you had after reading the passage. _____

_____

2. Why do you have this opinion? Write two sentences. Include a reason and a linking word from the word bank in each sentence.

also	and	because	but	or

_____

_____

_____

_____

3. Write a paragraph using this information. Include your opinion, two reasons, and a concluding sentence.

_____

_____

_____

_____

_____

_____

_____

❑ I can write about a topic or a book and tell how I feel about it.
❑ I can make good word choices when writing.

As characters try to solve their problems, a story develops, and other things begin to happen. This is called the **plot** of the story. For example, in *The Wizard of Oz*, Dorothy meets three good friends and faces a wicked witch as part of the plot. The plot is often divided into three parts: the beginning, the middle, and the end.

The pictures below tell a story. What does the story look like it is about?

Write the main idea.

1. Main idea _____

Write what happens at the beginning, the middle, and the end. Then, write a concluding sentence that includes your thoughts about the pictures.

2. Beginning _____

_____

3. Middle _____

_____

4. End _____

_____

5. Conclusion _____

_____

☐ **I can write to inform about a topic with facts and other details.**
☐ **I can make good word choices when writing.**

Read the passage.

Fire Station Field Trip

Today, our class took a field trip to the fire station. First, we met Captain James. He showed us the big fire trucks. The fire trucks, or fire engines, have many switches and valves. They have many compartments that hold the equipment and tools used to fight fires and help in emergencies.

We saw the large hoses the firefighters use to put out, or extinguish, fires. We saw the tall ladders the firefighters climb to reach high places. We saw the uniforms the firefighters wear when they fight fires. We got to put on their coats, pants, boots, and hats. The clothes that firefighters wear are big and heavy. Danny fell over because of the weight of the clothes!

Then, we got to see where the firefighters live when they are on duty. Inside the fire station, there are beds, showers, and a kitchen. The firefighters take turns shopping for food and cooking meals.

Suddenly, we heard a loud siren. The siren meant that there was an emergency. The firefighters quickly jumped on their fire trucks and drove away. It was interesting to see the fire station and learn about the job of a firefighter.

❑ I can read and understand informational text.

1. Recall reading about the field trip to the fire station on page 58. Write a complete sentence about a field trip you went on before.

_____

_____

2. Write three events from your field trip in order.
   A. First, _____

   _____

   B. Then, _____

   _____

   C. After, _____

   _____

3. How did you feel about the field trip? Write a complete sentence.

_____

_____

4. Would you recommend the field trip to a friend's class? Why or why not? Write a complete sentence.

_____

_____

Write your answers to numbers 1 to 4 in a paragraph on a separate sheet of paper or on a computer. Include the main idea, three events in order, a sentence about your feelings, and a sentence to conclude your paragraph.

☐ **I can write a detailed story that has a clear sequence of events.**
☐ **I can make good word choices when writing.**

Brainstorming a Story

A *brainstorm* is a group of ideas that are about one topic. Writing a brainstorm helps you recognize important details of a topic.

1. Complete the brainstorm below. The topic, *Story*, is in the circle. The lines are for your story ideas. What would you like to write about? Be creative!

Story

2. Circle the story idea you like best. Write it. _____

_____

3. Why did you choose this story idea? Write a complete sentence. _____

_____

_____

4. Write a list of characters that will appear in your story. Include at least two characters.

_____

_____

❑ **I can stick to a topic.**

Outlining a Story

A story includes characters, setting, and plot. These are called story elements. Follow the steps below and use page 60 to outline, or plan, a story from your brainstorm.

1. Plan at least two characters. Write their names and three words to describe each one.

Character 1	Character 2
A. _____	A. _____
B. _____	B. _____
C. _____	C. _____
Character 3	Character 4
A. _____	A. _____
B. _____	B. _____
C. _____	C. _____

2. Where will your story take place? Write about the setting. _____

_____

_____

3. What problem will your characters face? _____

_____

_____

4. How will they solve the problem? _____

_____

❑ **I can stick to a topic.**

Drafting a Story

Use your outline on page 61 to draft your story. How will your plot unfold? Plan a beginning, a middle, and an end to your story.

Beginning

_____

_____

_____

_____

Middle

_____

_____

_____

_____

End

_____

_____

_____

_____

❑ I can stick to a topic.

Revising

When you edit to make your writing better, you **revise** it. It is helpful to revise writing to be sure it is free of mistakes. Revising makes you a better writer. Look at page 62 and complete the first checklist below by yourself. Then, have a friend look at page 62 and complete the second checklist. This is called **peer editing**.

Revision Points	Notes—Writing I Can Fix	Checked ✔
1. I used complete sentences.		
2. I used capital letters at the beginning of sentences.		
3. I used ending punctuation.		
4. I spelled all of my words correctly.		
5. I wrote legibly.		
6. I have story elements.		

Revision Points	Notes—Writing That Can Be Fixed	Checked ✔
1. The student used complete sentences.		
2. The student used capital letters at the beginning of sentences.		
3. The student used ending punctuation.		
4. The student spelled all of the words correctly.		
5. The student wrote legibly.		
6. The student has story elements.		

❏ **I can revise my writing and edit my work.**
❏ **I can get support from peers with my writing.**

Final Copy

When a peer or adult revises a draft, and it has been fixed, it is ready to become a final draft, or **final copy**. A final copy can be written on paper or typed on a computer. Write your story from page 62. Make sure to consider the suggestions you and your peer made on page 63. Use the space below to write your story or type it on a computer. Make sure to include a title.

_____

_____

_____

_____

_____

_____

_____

_____

_____

_____

_____

❑ I can revise my writing.
❑ I can use technology to write and publish my work.

Read the letter. Imagine Luke's voice as you read the letter. Then, answer the questions and write a letter of your own.

June 5, 2014

Dear Grandma and Grandpa,

What's happening? I'm just hanging out. Today is the first day of my summer vacation. I have some amazing things planned this summer. Later today, my friend Miguel is coming over. We're going to ride our bikes. Tomorrow, I start swimming lessons. Mom said that in two weeks, we are going to visit you. I can't wait! Can we go to the park with the water slides? I had a blast last year when we were there. Also, I would like to go fishing. This year, I'm going to catch the biggest fish. You'll have to buy a new pan to cook it in, because I don't think the pans you have are big enough! Well, I have to split. Catch you later!

Love,
Luke

1. Do you write letters to family or friends? _____

2. On a separate sheet of paper, write a short letter to a friend to tell them what you did last night. Remember the exact sequence of events.

3. What is a difference between a letter in the mail and an email? Write a complete sentence.

_____

_____

☐ **I can write a detailed story that has a clear sequence of events.**
☐ **I can compare formal and informal uses of English.**

Use the letter on page 65 to answer the questions.

1. Who is the letter to? _____

2. Who is the letter from? _____

3. Name two things that Luke is going to do this summer. _____

_____

Language between family and friends often includes slang words and phrases. Slang words are informal words that should not be used in formal speech or writing. Draw a line to connect each slang word or phrase to its meaning.

4. What's happening?   go

5. hanging out   See you soon!

6. blast   How are you?

7. split   relaxing

8. Catch you later!   fun

9. On the next page, you are going write a letter. Make a list of possible people who you will write to.

_____

10. Write three events you might write about in the order they happened.

_____

_____

_____

☐ **I can write a detailed story that has a clear sequence of events.**
☐ **I can read informal and formal writing.**

1. Write a letter to someone you listed on page 66. Look at Luke's letter on page 65 and reread it if you need ideas.

Dear _____,

_____

_____

_____

_____

_____

_____

Love,

_____

2. Find a partner to review your work, using the checklist below.

The student included a greeting at the beginning.	
The student listed things he or she did.	
The student used feeling in the writing.	
I can "hear" the writer's voice.	
The student included a closing sentence.	

☐ **I can write a detailed story that has a clear sequence of events.**
☐ **I can collaborate with peers.**

Read the checklist on page 67 to see if you were missing anything in your letter. Rewrite your letter and make sure to revise it. Write it below, type it on a computer, or type it in an email.

_____

_____

_____

_____

_____

_____

_____

_____

_____

_____

❏ **I can use technology to write and publish my work.**

You are going to research a famous person in sports. To prepare, read about Michael Jordan in the **biography** below. A biography is a written history of a person's life. Then, answer the questions.

Michael Jordan was born on February 17, 1963, in Brooklyn, New York. He grew up in North Carolina and attended school there. His father built a basketball court in the backyard of their house. Michael and his four brothers and sisters played there.

When Michael was in high school, he played baseball. He did not make the basketball team and was very disappointed. He kept practicing basketball. By the next year, he had grown four inches! He finally made the team and went on to play in college.

Michael played so well in college that he was a professional basketball player and later an Olympic basketball player. He played for the Chicago Bulls from 1984 until 1993. Then, he decided to play baseball but soon returned to the Chicago Bulls in 1995. He is known as one of the greatest basketball players of all time.

1. What is the main idea of the biography?
   A. Michael was one of the highest-paid basketball players.
   B. Michael is one of the greatest basketball players of all time.
   C. Michael played for the Chicago Bulls.

2. What is Michael best known for?
   A. playing baseball
   B. playing basketball
   C. being born in Brooklyn, New York

3. Write *T* for each sentence that is true. Write *F* for each sentence that is false.

   _____ Michael was born in Chicago.

   _____ Michael played for the Chicago Bulls.

   _____ Michael lived in North Carolina while growing up.

❑ **I can research for a writing project.**

2.W.7, 2.W.8

1. Write the name of a sport you enjoy. _____

2. Research a person who plays this sport. He or she may be a professional athlete or just a friend. If you choose a professional athlete, look for information about his or her life in books, magazines, newspapers, or on the Internet. You may do research in a library, the classroom, or at home. If you choose a friend or a person you know, ask about his or her life in person or on the phone.

3. Gather information about the person's life. Complete the research organizer below.

Name of athlete	
Date of birth	
Place of birth	
Childhood information	
Sport played	
Team name	
Known for (famous fact)	

4. Why does he or she play the sport? Write a complete sentence.

_____

_____

_____

5. Write a fact you learned.

_____

_____

❑ **I can write and record research.**
❑ **I can gather information for research.**

You are going to research your favorite place. To prepare, read the story.

Brianna's Favorite Place

Brianna lives in New Foundland, Canada. Today, she is visiting her favorite place, high on a steep cliff that overlooks the ocean. She likes to watch the fishing boats bob like corks in the blue water. She listens to the sounds of the seagulls as they look for food. She admires the beauty of the tall lighthouse. She laughs as she watches the whales play. Brianna lies on her back. She clearly sees animals in the clouds. Brianna loves to feel the mist from the ocean against her face. It is a peaceful day.

All of a sudden, a huge wave swiftly crashes into the shore. The fishing boats start coming to port as fast as they can. The clouds quickly darken. A strong wind begins to blow. A foghorn cries out. It warns the sailors that a storm is coming. The waves rapidly get bigger and bigger.

As the storm comes in, Brianna is glad that she is high above the angry ocean. She takes one last look at the beautiful white-capped waves. Then, she runs home.

1. Adverbs are words that describe verbs. They make writing more interesting and detailed. Write the adverb from the story that describes each verb.

   A. _____ sees

   B. _____ crashes

   C. _____ darken

   D. _____ get

2. Adjectives are words that describe nouns. They liven up writing. Write the adjective from the story that describes each noun.

   A. _____ cliff

   B. _____ water

   C. _____ day

   D. _____ wave

   E. _____ wind

   F. _____ ocean

☐ **I can do research for a writing project.**
☐ **I can use adjectives and adverbs appropriately.**

1. Where is your favorite place?_____

2. Why is it your favorite place? Write a complete sentence. _____

   _____

   _____

3. Research your favorite place. Read about your favorite place in books, magazines, newspapers, or on the Internet. You may do research in a library, the classroom, or at home.

4. Gather facts from your research. Make a list of facts about your favorite place.

| My favorite place is _____ . |
| Fact 1: |
| Fact 2: |
| Fact 3: |
| Fact 4: |
| Fact 5: |

❑ I can research and write about a topic.
❑ I can gather information and record facts.

A **collective noun** names a group of things, or members. Write the collective noun from the word bank that best completes each sentence.

army	band	crew	family	group	staff	team

1. Tony went on a _____ vacation with his aunts, uncles, and cousins.

2. The boat _____ had to wash the deck and clean the sails.

3. Luis practiced with his baseball _____ at the field.

4. The _____ of teachers were in the cafeteria having a meeting.

5. Mario's rock _____ played music at the show.

6. The students got together to make a study _____ before for the test.

7. The _____ wore special green-and-brown outfits at boot camp.

❏ **I can identify collective nouns.**
❏ **I can write collective nouns in sentences.**

A **plural noun** is more than one thing and usually ends in the letter s, as in the word *books*. An **irregular plural noun** does not end like a regular plural noun. An irregular plural noun has spelling changes at the end of the word. Use the spelling rules to complete the tables.

Nouns	Rule	Irregular Plural Nouns
wolf		
leaf		
elf	Change *f* to *ve* and add *-s*	
shelf		
scarf		

Nouns	Rule	Irregular Plural Nouns
echo		
hero		
tomato	Change *o* to *oes*	
potato		
volcano		

© Carson-Dellosa • CD-104609

❑ **I can form and use most irregular plural nouns.**

Write a complete sentence with each reflexive pronoun in the word bank.

| herself | himself | itself | myself | ourselves | themselves |

1. _____

_____

2. _____

_____

3. _____

_____

4. _____

_____

5. _____

_____

6. _____

_____

☐ **I can use reflexive pronouns in my writing.**

A complete sentence has a subject, which is usually a noun. The subject is followed by a verb. Rearrange each complete sentence. Each sentence will still have a subject and a verb, but they will be in a different order.

Example: The boy watched the movie.
         The movie was watched by the boy.

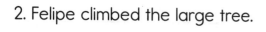

1. Tasha looked for her snow boots.

_____

_____

2. Felipe climbed the large tree.

_____

_____

3. Grandma cooked steak on the grill.

_____

_____

4. Connor did his homework at the kitchen table.

_____

_____

5. The girls counted the ducks in the pond.

_____

_____

❑ **I can write complete sentences.**
❑ **I can rearrange complete sentences.**

Editors are people who edit and revise written work. Their jobs are to make sure that all sentences in newspapers or magazines are correct. Editors also fix sentences in books and online websites. Pretend that you are an editor. Revise and rewrite the sentences. Each sentence has three errors.

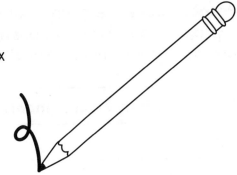

1. the lady crossed the stret with her new puppy

_____

2. marc wanted to play outsid, but it was raining

_____

3. cynthia waited for the mail carrier two arrive

_____

4. gene rode to the stor on his bike

_____

5. will you tak us to the park today

_____

6. yolanda took car of the children yesterday

_____

7. when is Mom going to com home

_____

8. i tried to find my missing sock four an hour

_____

9. maria laughed at the funy TV show

_____

10. Mrs. vale needed to mak copies for her class

_____

☐ **I can follow the rules about words and sentences.**

Proper nouns are nouns that need to start with capital letters. A person's name is a proper noun. Holidays, businesses and product names, and geographic names are also proper nouns. Rewrite the nouns so that they are proper.

Holiday Nouns (incorrect)	Holiday Proper Nouns (correct)
boxing day	
groundhog day	
canada day	
new year's day	
mother's day	

Businesses/Product Nouns (incorrect)	Businesses/Product Proper Nouns (correct)
mike and henry's	
sabatino's restaurant	
dress buy	
danny's tea shop	
yogurt yummies	

Geographic Names (incorrect)	Geographic Proper Nouns (correct)
india	
tennessee	
japan	
atlantic	
canada	

❑ I can recognize proper nouns.
❑ I can capitalize proper nouns.

Commas are used in greetings and closings of letters. A comma signals a pause. When a comma is used after a greeting, it lets the reader know the body of the letter is starting. When a comma is used after a closing, it lets the reader know the letter is ending.

Read each letter. Add a comma after the greeting and the closing of each letter.

Dear Aunt Jill

   How are you doing? I can't wait to meet you! Mom said you are such a fun person to be around. Do you like crafts like I do? We should go to a pottery studio to make bowls or string some beads together to make jewelry. Maybe we could even make special bracelets for each other! I look forward to meeting you in two weeks. Stay well!

Sincerely
Beth

Dear Norris

   Thank you for coming to my birthday party. I enjoyed your company. I hope you had fun swimming in the pool and eating hamburgers. The toy you gave me is one of my favorites. How did you know I like tow trucks? You are a great friend. Come over again sometime soon!

Your friend
Logan

MAIL

☐ **I can use commas in greetings and closings.**

Name_____

Read the story. Complete the chart.

The Birthday Present Mix-Up

Today is Rachel's birthday. She invited four friends to her party. Each friend brought a present. Rachel's little brother mixed up the tags on the presents. Can you use the clues to put the tags on the right presents?

- Kelly's present has flowered wrapping paper and a bow.
- Kate's present is square and has a bow.
- Megan forgot the bow on her present.
- Lisa's present has striped wrapping paper.

Write an X in the correct box when you know a girl *did not* bring a present. Write an O when you know a girl *did* bring a present.

Kate				
Kelly				
Lisa				
Megan				

An **apostrophe** is used to show possession. Circle the word that needs an apostrophe in each sentence. Write the word correctly.

1. Rachels brother is three years old. _____

2. Kates present has a big bow. _____

3. My brothers friend spent the night. _____

4. Each presents tag was missing. _____

5. Lisas present has striped paper. _____

❑ **I can use an apostrophe.**

Spelling patterns help us identify which letters to use when spelling words. Use the word on the top of each column to help you add similar words with the same pattern.

ca**ge**	ba**dge**	b**oi**l	t**oy**

phone	**kn**ife	fa**ce**	va**se**

gem	**j**ewel	li**ft**	cli**ff**

☐ **I can use spelling patterns to write words.**

Name_____

A **dictionary** is a book of words and their meanings. A word you look up is called an **entry word**. Guide words are found in the top corners of each dictionary page. The word on the right is the very last word on that page. Guide words are helpful in guiding you to the word you need in a faster manner. You can flip through the dictionary, looking only at guide words until you find the page where your word would fit.

The entry words in the word bank are out of order. Write them in alphabetical order under the correct guide words.

| lamp | loud | lane | locket | learn | lot |
| low | large | lion | lobster | listen | love |

lamb

1. _____

3. _____

least

2. _____

4. _____

licorice

5. _____

7. _____

loose

6. _____

8. _____

lost

9. _____

11. _____

lucky

10. _____

12. _____

☐ **I can look up words in the dictionary.**

When you come to a word you do not know, sometimes you can determine the meaning from **context clues** in the sentence.

Example: The cowboy tried to *calm* the horses *after the loud thunder ended.* (The words *after the loud thunder ended* give you a clue about the meaning of *calm.* Calm means to "settle down.")

Use context clues to help you choose each bold word's meaning.

1. The blue paint turned a **pale** color when I added water to it.
   A. bright
   B. light
   C. green

2. Dad sharpened the **blade** on the lawn mower.
   A. machine part for cutting
   B. handle
   C. wheel

3. Mom likes to relax on the **sofa** after she takes us swimming.
   A. bike
   B. stairs
   C. couch

4. Would you like a large or small **slice** of watermelon?
   A. plate
   B. piece
   C. picnic

5. Prairie dogs sit on **mounds** to help them see danger coming.
   A. their tails
   B. small hills
   C. chairs

6. The aquarium has many **rare** fish that would be hard to see anywhere else.
   A. special
   B. large
   C. scary

❑ **I can find the meaning of a word in a sentence.**
❑ **I can use context clues to determine the meaning of a new word.**

Sometimes, context clues, along with your own ideas, will help you make a good guess at a word's meaning. Use context clues to help you choose each bold word's meaning.

1. Most small children are **forbidden** to cross the street without an adult.
   A. allowed
   B. not allowed
   C. forced

2. Tracy buttoned her **cardigan** to keep warm at the game.
   A. sweater
   B. pajamas
   C. boots

3. The autumn morning **dew** left the playground damp.
   A. clumps of snow
   B. pieces of ice
   C. drops of water

4. Dad likes to **relax** after he takes us biking.
   A. jump
   B. rest
   C. sleep

5. Our team must be **united** if we want to win the championship.
   A. working together
   B. awake
   C. dressed up

6. I remember that type of butterfly by its **distinct** markings.
   A. yellow
   B. special
   C. dirty

7. The balloon **burst** as it brushed against the brick wall.
   A. flew higher
   B. got away
   C. popped

8. Some American Indians made their **dwellings** in rock cliffs.
   A. shoes
   B. blankets
   C. homes

❑ I can find the meaning of a word in a sentence.
❑ I can use context clues to determine the meaning of a new word.

A **compound word** is made by joining two or more words to make a new word with a new meaning.

Example: *fire + works = fireworks*

Complete each sentence with a compound word from the word bank.

| backward | campground | cartwheels | copperhead | daybreak | grandfather |
| hairstylist | landmark | lighthouse | snowflakes | stepladder | sunflower |

1. The Washington Monument is a well-known_____ .

2. The teacher said to take one step _____.

3. My mother's dad is my _____.

4. It was dark and foggy, so the sailor was happy to see the

   _____.

5. I read in my science book that _____ snakes are venomous.

6. In the gym, they showed us how to do _____.

7. We pitched our tent at a beautiful new _____.

8. When the first _____ fall, we know that winter is on its way.

9. Mom must use a _____ to reach the top kitchen cabinets.

10. The lady has an appointment with the _____ every six weeks.

11. Many birds and animals look for _____ seeds to eat.

12. Roosters usually awaken at _____.

❑ **I can determine the meaning of compound words by understanding the meanings of the individual words.**

The meaning of a word you look up in a dictionary is called the **definition**. If the word has more than one meaning, the definitions are numbered.

Use the dictionary entries to answer the questions.

cream \'krEm\ *noun, plural* **creams**
the yellowish-white part of milk (Butter is made from *cream*.)

crook \'kruk\ *noun, plural* **crooks**
1. a bent part; curve (My umbrella was in the *crook* of my arm.) 2. a shepherd's staff with a hook at the top 3. a person who is not honest.

cry \'krI\ *verb* **cried, crying**
1. to shed tears; weep (Don't make the baby *cry*.) 2. to call out loudly; shout (I heard the people near the burning building *cry* for help.)

cute \'kyüt\ *adjective* **cuter, cutest**
delightful or pretty (That is a very *cute* puppy.)

¹· **dash** \dash\ *verb* **dashed, dashing**
1. to move fast; rush (If I am late, I *dash* to my classroom.) 2. to destroy or ruin (If I hurt my ankle, it will *dash* my hopes of running in the race.)

²· **dash** *noun* 1. a fast movement or sudden rush (I made a *dash* for the waiting bus.) 2. a small amount

1. Which definition best fits the word *cry* as it is used in this sentence?

    The little girl cried for her mother. Definition number _____

2. List other forms of the word *cute*. _____

3. Which part of speech is the word *cream*? _____

4. Which definition best fits the word *crook* as it is used in this sentence?

    The crook stole the diamond. Definition number _____

5. What is the definition of the word *dash* as a verb? _____

_____

❑ **I can use a dictionary to determine the meaning of a word.**

Word nuances are shades of differences. Nuances show a word's shades of meaning. You can change a word's meaning by saying it in a tone. Ending punctuation helps determine tone.

For example, if you say the word *fire*, it seems like a plain old noun. If you say the word *fire* as if it were a question (fire?), it sounds as if you are wondering about a fire. But, if you shout the word (fire!), then people may think something is in flames.

Find a partner. Take turns saying the listed words as statements, questions, or exclamations. Notice the difference in tone. How does each one make you feel or think? Write it in the table.

Word	Punctuation for Tone	Thoughts and Feelings
really	?	
really	!	
go	.	
go	!	
run	?	
run	!	
wait	.	
wait	!	

❑ I can understand nuances in words.
❑ I can use tone when speaking and writing.

Making real-world connections with words and knowing how words are used can make your writing stronger. If you can relate to words, you can use them better in your writing. It is also important to use your five senses (sight, hearing, smell, taste, and touch) when making a connection.

Use your five senses to complete the chart.

1. Describe foods that are spicy. How do they taste?	
2. Describe sandpaper. How does it feel?	
3. Describe the aroma of perfume. How does it smell?	
4. Describe the view from the top of a mountain. What does it look like?	
5. Describe the noises of a baby banging pots and pans. How does it sound?	

☐ I can make real-world connections between words and their use.

Many verbs are related. They have similar definitions but are slightly different. Verbs have shades of meaning.

Example: *toss, throw, hurl*

Tossing is gentle, throwing is firm, and hurling is rough.

Find a partner. Take turns performing the meaning of each word.

1. whisper   speak   shout

2. stroll   walk   jog

3. peek   look   stare

4. sip   drink   gulp

5. tap   touch   poke

Many adjectives are related. They have similar definitions but are slightly different. Adjectives have shades of meaning.

Example: *thin, slender, skinny, scrawny*

Draw lines to connect the related adjectives.

6. big   smelly

7. chilly   hot

8. boiling   dirty

9. dusty   huge

10. stinking   freezing

☐ **I can tell the differences between synonyms.**

Using adjectives and adverbs in writing helps it to be more interesting. Adjectives describe the nouns in sentences. Adverbs describe the verbs.

Underline the adjective in each sentence. Circle the adverb in each sentence.

1. The old boat quickly drifted to sea.

2. The lonely puppy truly needed an owner.

3. The happy children played loudly in the playroom.

4. Eboni quickly ran to the kitchen to make delicious cookies.

5. George patiently waited for his turn with the colorful toy.

6. Nicholas quietly tiptoed up the creaky staircase.

7. Simone easily finished her short homework assignment.

Write three sentences. Include an adjective and an adverb in each sentence.

8. _____

_____

9. _____

_____

10. _____

_____

❏ **I can use new words that I have learned.**
❏ **I can use adjectives and adverbs in my writing.**

Answer Key

Page 13
1. B; 2. A; 3. came; 4. said; 5. fed; 6. took; 7. went; 8. broke; 9. kept; 10. bit

Page 14
1. The moral of the story is to be happy with what you have. City Mouse—first, fourth, and sixth descriptions; Country Mouse—second, third, and fifth descriptions

Page 16
1. C; 2, C; 3. A; 4. B; 5. A; 6. one; 7. dear; 8. some; 9. two, to; 10. days

Page 17
1. Answers will vary but may include that Brandon realized his arm was broken, so he went to the doctor. 2. Answers will vary but may include that the doctor put a cast on Brandon's arm and told him his bones would grow back in place. 3. Answers will vary but may include that Matthew knew Brandon's arm was broken, and Matthew suggested playing tic-tac-toe instead of wall ball with Brandon at school.

Page 19
1. into; 2. on; 3. over; 4. down; 5. in; 6. hardest; 7. longest; 8. greenest; 9. freshest; 10. deepest; 11. smallest;

12. kindest; 13. fastest; 14. slowest; 15. highest

Page 20
1. The story begins with Nathan giving his mom a large gift. 2. The story ends with Mom giving Nathan a big hug. 3. the mother; 4. Nathan

Page 21
1. Manuel; 2. Joshua

Page 22
Drawings will vary. The first box should have beautiful forestry, and the second box should have a polluted environment.

Page 24
1. Answers will vary but may include that both stories have girls as the main characters. Both girls have slippers. 2. Answers will vary but may include that the two girls are different because they have different names. Yeh-Shen uses magic fish bones, and Cinderella has a fairy godmother.

Page 26
1. B; 2. F; 3. T; 4. F; 5. swim; 6. fly; 7. learn; 8. swing; 9. be; 10. have

Page 27
1. more than 850; 2. insects,

fruit, nectar; 3. more than 15 inches (38 cm) long; 4. mango, guava, cashew, clove, Brazil nut; 5. sonar-guided ears and mouths

Page 28
1. C; 2. B; 3. A

Page 29
1. B; 2. C; 3. A; 4. Answers will vary but may include that they are all about successful men who helped the United States.

Page 31
1. B; 2. A; 3. A; 4. B; 5. koalas; 6. marsupials; 7. pouches; 8. babies; 9. leaves

Page 32
1. D; 2. A; 3. B; 4. C

Page 33
1. The author's purpose is to compare and contrast old cars and new cars. 2. Both types of cars help people get around, are affordable, and use gas. Old cars had gas tanks under the front seats. Old cars needed hot water on cold days. Old cars could not go as fast as new cars can.

Page 35
1. A; 2. fraternal and identical; 3. look the same; 4. look different;

Answer Key

5.

Description	Chris	William
born on December 22	X	X
curly red hair and blue eyes		X
straight brown hair and green eyes	X	
missing two front teeth	X	
good ball player	X	X

Page 36
1. Answers will vary but may include that germs make people sick. 2. Answers will vary but may include that germs can get into the bodies of others in many ways.

Page 38
1. It protects the head. 2. They protect the hands. 3. They both deal with safety and protection of our bodies. 4. They deal with safety of different body parts (head vs. hands). 5. toss/throw; 6. clutch/grab; 7. slam/close; 8. thin/slender; 9. small/tiny; 10. large/gigantic

Page 39
1. recording sheet; 2. edited writing; 3. Thursday; 4. math; 5. No assignment is due. 6. Wednesday; 7. Friday; 8. rough draft

Page 40
4, 2, 6, 3, 1, 5

Page 41
1. A; 2. C; 3. A

Page 42
1. wing; 2. bank; 3. sand; 4. scold; 5. cement; 6. couch; 7. trend; 8. months; 9. sprint; 10. lungs; 11. pink; 12. squash

Page 43
1. cup; 2. dot; 3. leg; 4. fan; 5. mop; 6. lips; 7. pig; 8. net; 9. hat; 10. truck; Words will vary but may include lip, not, bus.

Page 44
1. cape; 2. cake; 3. bride; 4. airplane; 5. bone; 6. kite; 7. rake; 8. pipe; 9. mule; 10. cone; 11. cane; 12. tape

Page 45
1. sleep; 2. rain; 3. soap; 4. pail; 5. boat; 6. beach; 7. see

Page 46
1. cloud; 2. point; 3. tower; 4. boil; 5. screw; 6. chew; 7. growl; 8. soil; 9. jewel; 10. crown; 11. mouth; 12. house

Page 47
1. 2, 2; 2. 1, 1; 3. 1, 1; 4. 2, 2; 5. 3, 3; 6. 2, 2; 7. 2, 2; 8. 3, 3; 9. 1, 1; 10. 1, 1; 1 syllable: three, nail, grape, sweet; 2 syllables: apron, window, playful, lady; 3 syllables: relaxing, favorite

Page 48
1. submarine: underwater vehicle; 2. exit: to leave; 3. undo: to take apart or redo: to do again; 4. review: to check again; 5. playful: to be full of play, lively or player: one who plays; 6. hopeless: without hope or hopeful: full of hope; 7. worker: one who works; 8. wooden: made of wood

Page 49
1. car; 2. first; 3. fur; 4. bird; 5. after; 6. dark; 7. stars

Page 50
1. whole; 2. mail; 3. prince; 4. Would; 5. rose; 6. rains; 7. paws; 8. flour; 9. hair; 10. scent

Page 51
1. The blanket was covered in ants. 2. They moved to a picnic table. 3. Jayden couldn't find his shoes. 4. He looked for them and found Michael wearing them.

Page 52
1–2. Answers will vary.

Page 53
1–3. Answers will vary.

Page 54
1. C; 2. B; 3. A; 4. B; 5–8. Answers will vary but should include adjectives and/or prepositional phrases.

Answer Key

Page 55
1–3. Answers will vary but may include that American Indians use dance to express themselves. The Fancy Dance includes dancers with feathers. The Hoop Dance includes dancers with hoops to show patterns in nature. 4-6. Answers will vary but may include that the Fancy Dance is fast and colorful. The Hoop Dance is the most difficult dance. Butterflies have peaceful lives. 7. Answers will vary.

Page 56
1. Answers will vary. 2. Answers will vary but should include two linking words (one in each sentence). 3. Answers will vary.

Page 57
1. The boy made a mess. 2. The boy spills his milk. 3. The boy cleans it up. 4. The boy gets a hug from his mother. 5. He cleaned it up and is happy now.

Page 59
1–4. Answers will vary based on students' personal experiences with field trips.

Page 60
1–4. Answers will vary based on students' brainstorms.

Page 61
1–4. Answers will vary based on students' characters.

Page 62
Answers will vary based on page 61.

Page 63
Answers will vary based on students' personal and peer writing reviews.

Page 64
Answers will vary because of story outlined on page 62.

Page 65
1. Answers will vary. 2. Answers will vary. 3. Answers will vary but may include that an email is electronic, and a letter in the mail is delivered by a mail carrier.

Page 66
1. Grandma and Grandpa; 2. Luke; 3. Answers will vary but may include that Luke will be fishing, swimming, and cooking. 4. How are you? 5. relaxing; 6. fun; 7. go; 8. See you soon! 9. Answers will vary. 10. Answers will vary.

Page 67
Answers will vary.

Page 68
Answers will vary.

Page 69
1. B; 2. B; 3. F, T, T

Page 70
1–5. Answers will vary.

Page 71
1. A. clearly; B. swiftly; C. quickly; D. rapidly; 2. A. steep; B. blue; C. peaceful; D. huge; E. strong; F. angry

Page 72
1–4. Answers will vary.

Page 73
1. family; 2. crew; 3. team; 4. staff; 5. band; 6. group; 7. army

Page 74
wolves, leaves, elves, shelves, scarves; echoes, heroes, tomatoes, potatoes, volcanoes

Page 75
1–6. Answers will vary.

Page 76
1. The snow boots were looked for by Tasha. 2. The large tree was climbed by Felipe. 3. The steak on the grill was cooked by Grandma. 4. At the kitchen table, Connor did his

Answer Key

homework. 5. The ducks in the pond were counted by the girls.

Page 77
1. The lady crossed the street with her new puppy. 2. Marc wanted to play outside, but it was raining. 3. Cynthia waited for the mail carrier to arrive. 4. Gene rode to the store on his bike. 5. Will you take us to the park today? 6. Yolanda took care of the children yesterday. 7. When is Mom going to come home? 8. I tried to find my missing sock for an hour. 9. Maria laughed at the funny TV show. 10. Mrs. Vale needed to make copies for her class.

Page 78
Boxing Day; Groundhog Day; Canada Day; New Year's Day; Mother's Day

Mike and Henry's; Sabatino's Restaurant; Dress Buy; Danny's Tea Shop; Yogurt Yummies

India; Tennessee; Japan; Atlantic; Canada

Page 79
A comma is needed after each greeting and closing.

Page 80

	Gift 1	Gift 2	Gift 3	Gift 4
Kate	O	X	X	X
Kelly	X	O	X	X
Lisa	X	X	X	O
Megan	X	X	O	X

1. Rachel's; 2. Kate's; 3. brother's; 4. present's; 5. Lisa's

Page 81
Answers will vary but may include sage, page, wage; edge, smudge, wedge; coil, foil, toil; boy, coy, Roy; phase, Phil, photo; knit, knot, know; lace, place, race; base, case, nose; gentle, germ, giraffe; Jack, Jenny, jump; gift, raft, rift; stuff, off, whiff.

Page 82
1. lamp, lane, large, learn; 2. lion, listen, lobster, locket; 3. lot, loud, love, low

Page 83
1. B; 2. A; 3. C; 4. B; 5. B; 6. A

Page 84
1. B; 2. A; 3. C; 4. B; 5. A; 6. B; 7. C; 8. C

Page 85
1. landmark; 2. backward; 3. grandfather; 4. lighthouse; 5. copperhead; 6. cartwheels; 7. campground; 8. snowflakes; 9. stepladder; 10. hairstylist; 11. sunflower; 12. daybreak

Page 86
1. 2; 2. cuter, cutest; 3. noun; 4. 3; 5. to move fast; rush

Page 87
Answers will vary.

Page 88
1–5. Answers will vary.

Page 89
1–5. Answers will vary. 6. big/huge; 7. chilly/freezing; 8. boiling/hot; 9. dusty/dirty; 10. stinking/smelly

Page 90
1. (underlined) old, (circled) quickly; 2. (underlined) lonely, (circled) truly; 3. (underlined) happy, (circled) loudly; 4. (circled) quickly, (underlined) delicious; 5. (circled) patiently, (underlined) colorful; 6. (circled) quietly, (underlined) creaky; 7. (circled) easily, (underlined) short; 8–10. Answers will vary.

Notes

Notes